Double Seventh Day

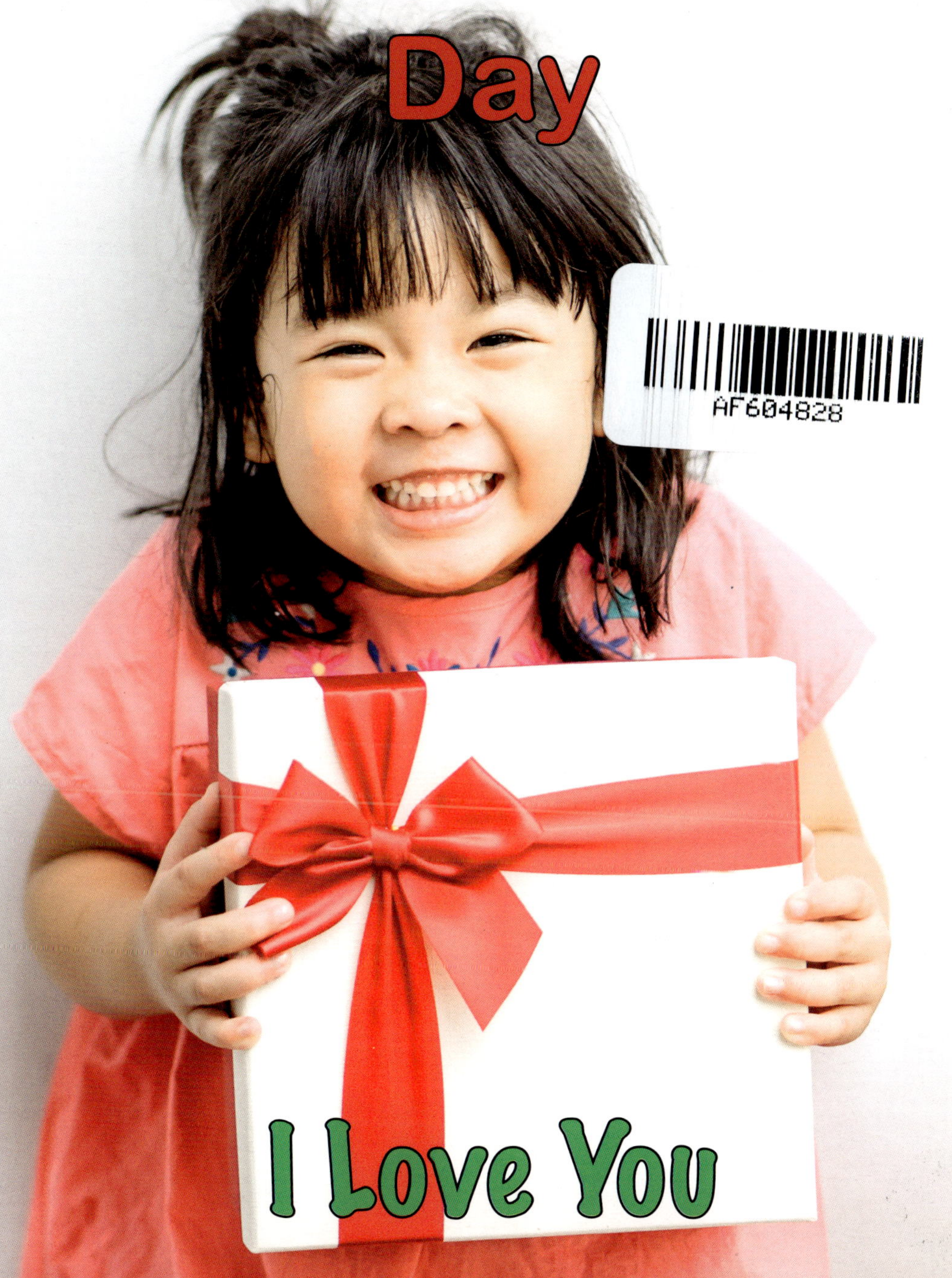

AF604828

I like to give flowers.

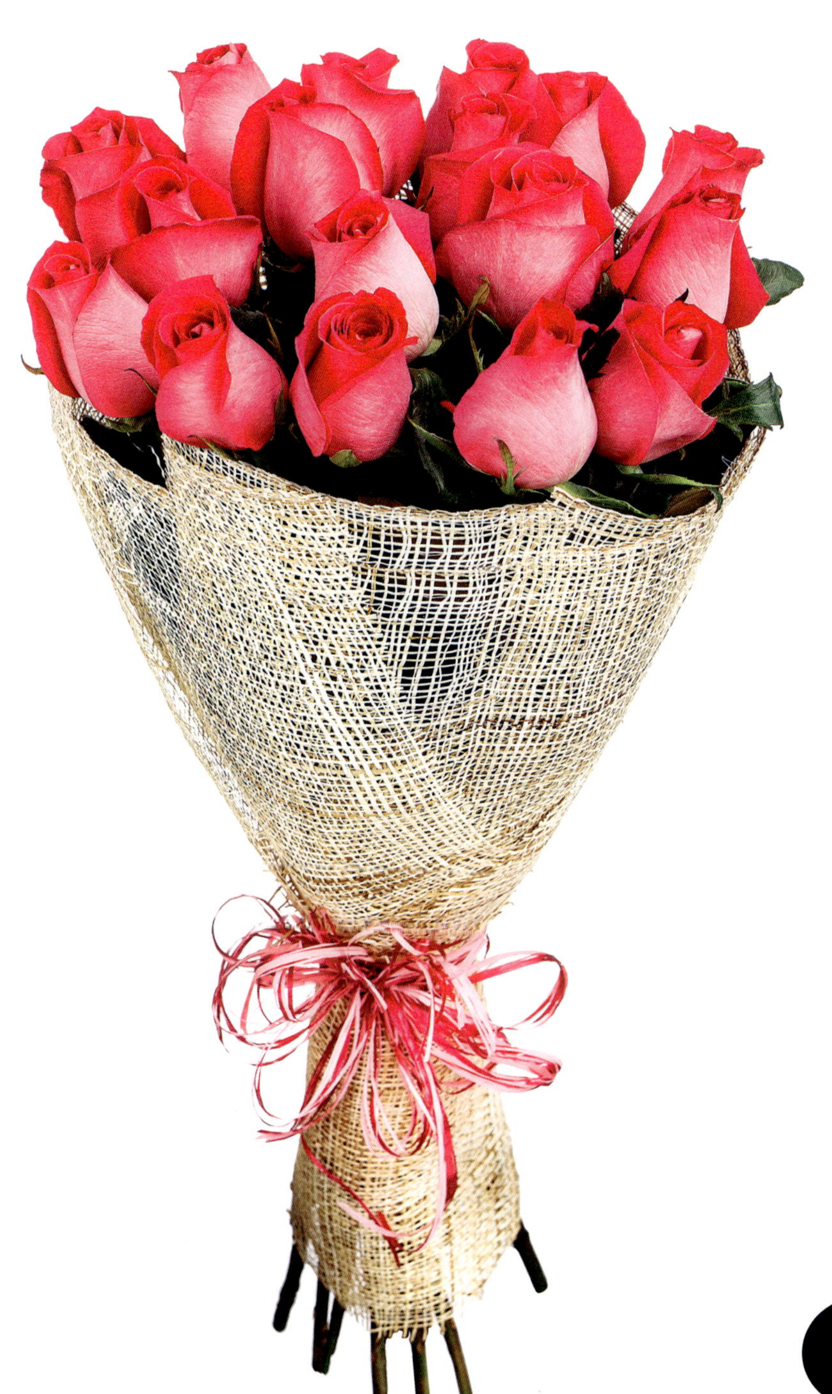

I like to give chocolates.

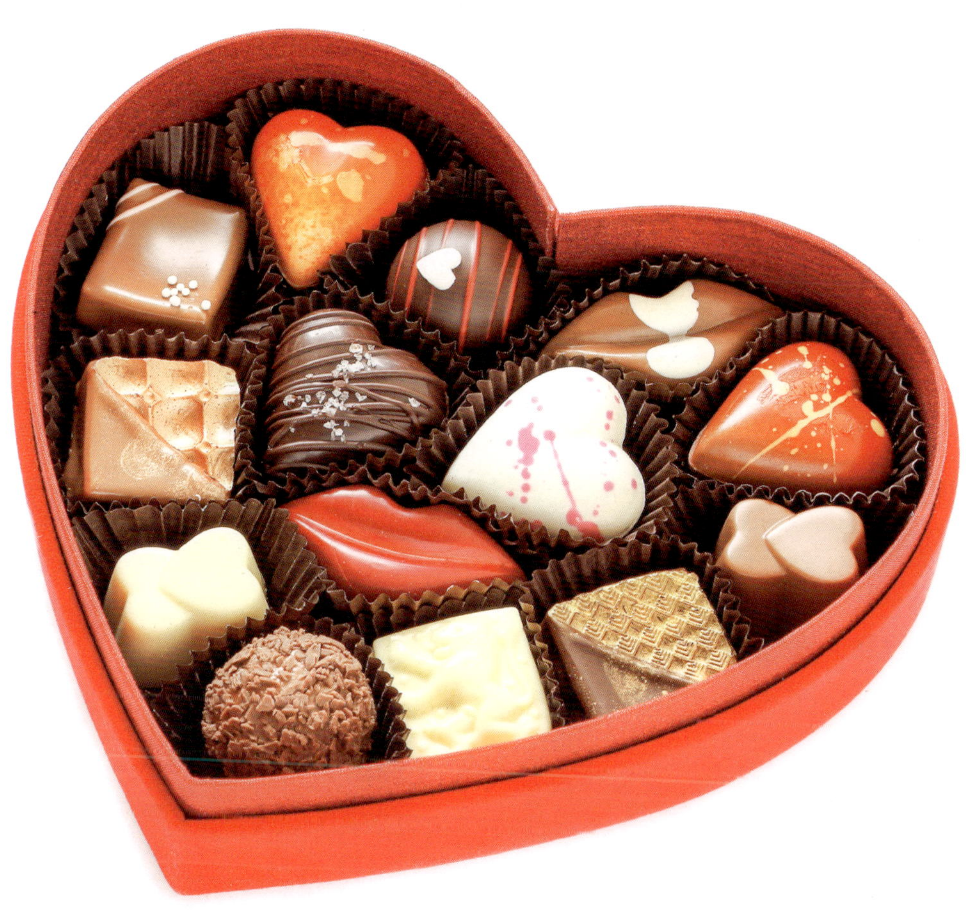

I like to give lollies.

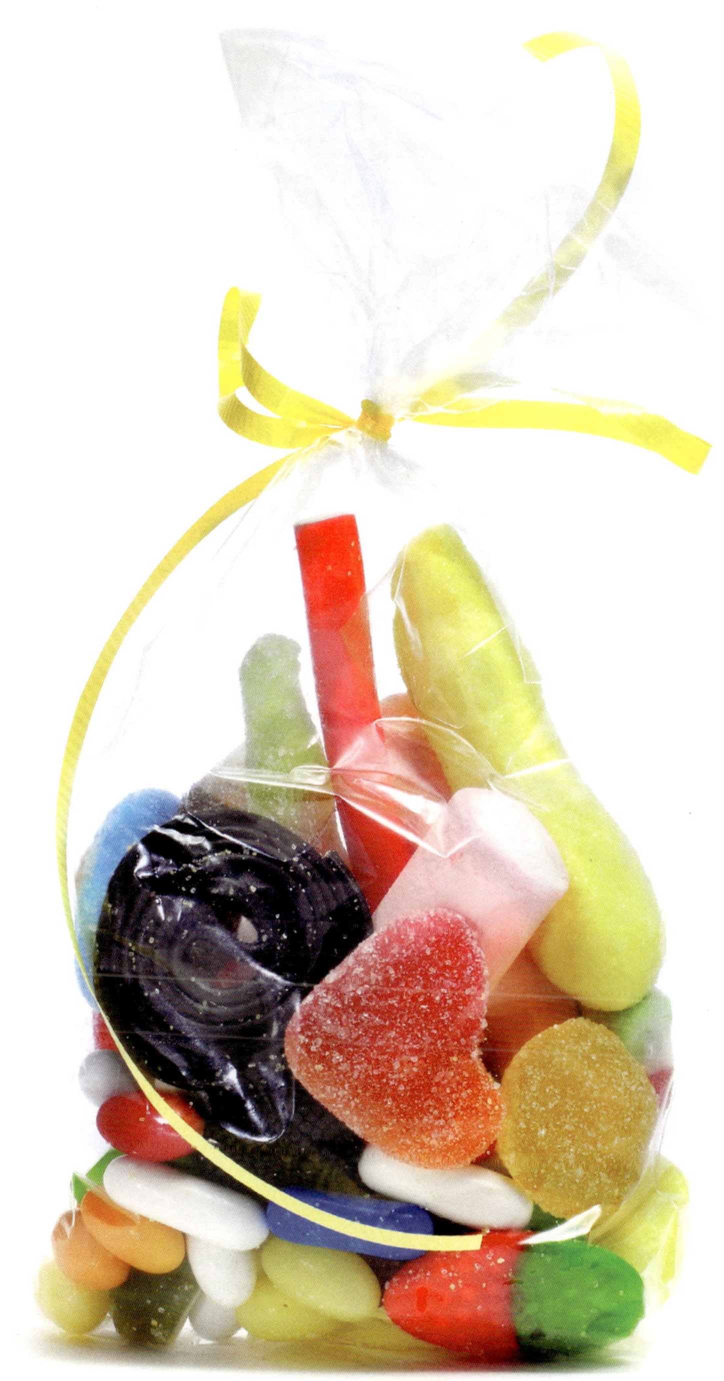

I like to give cup cakes.

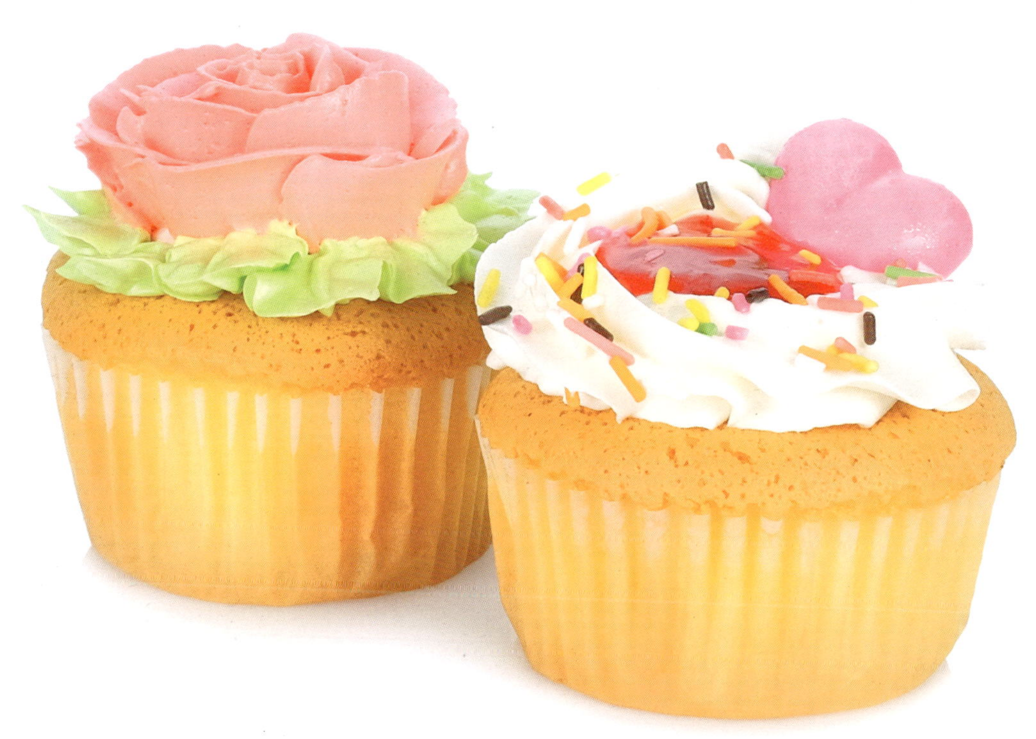

I like to give balloons.

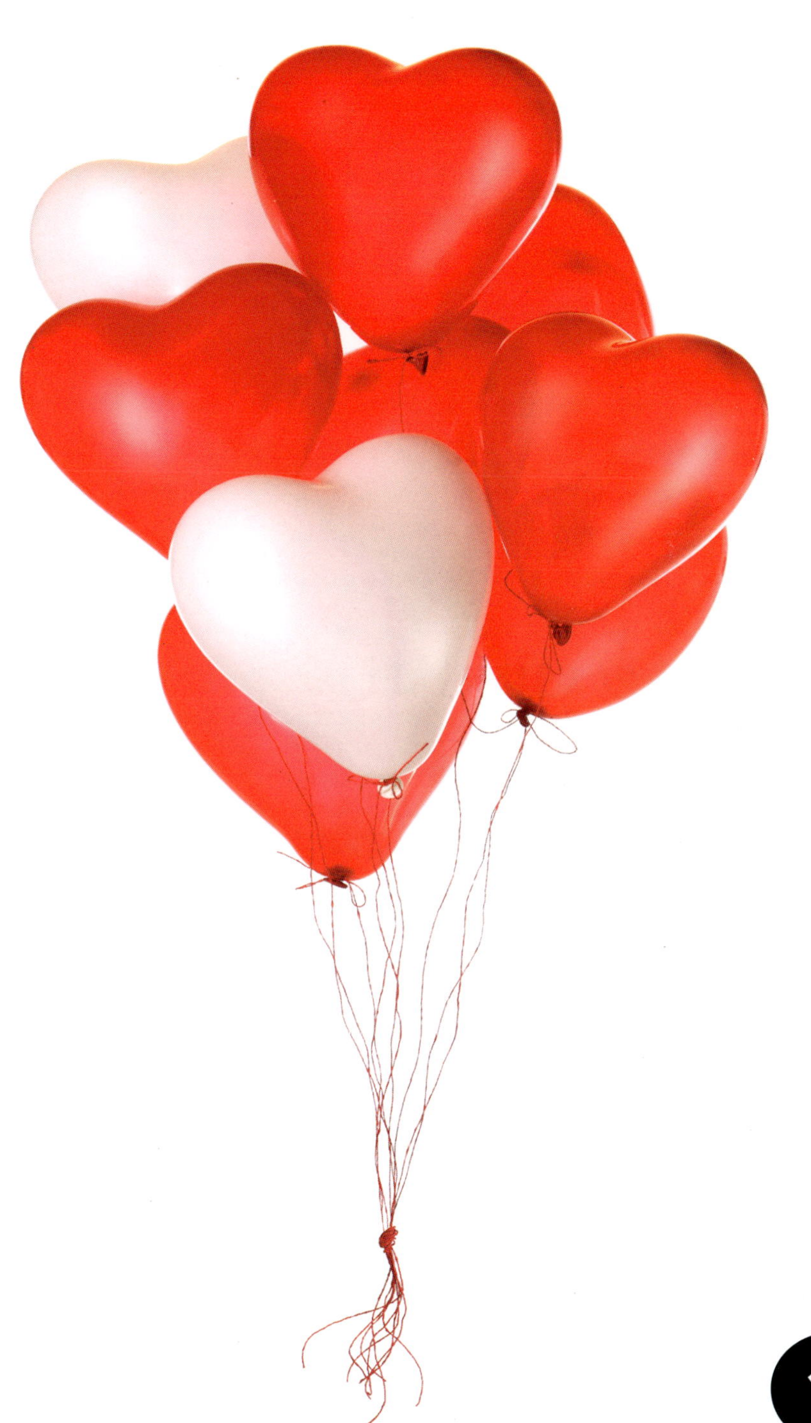

I like to give toys.

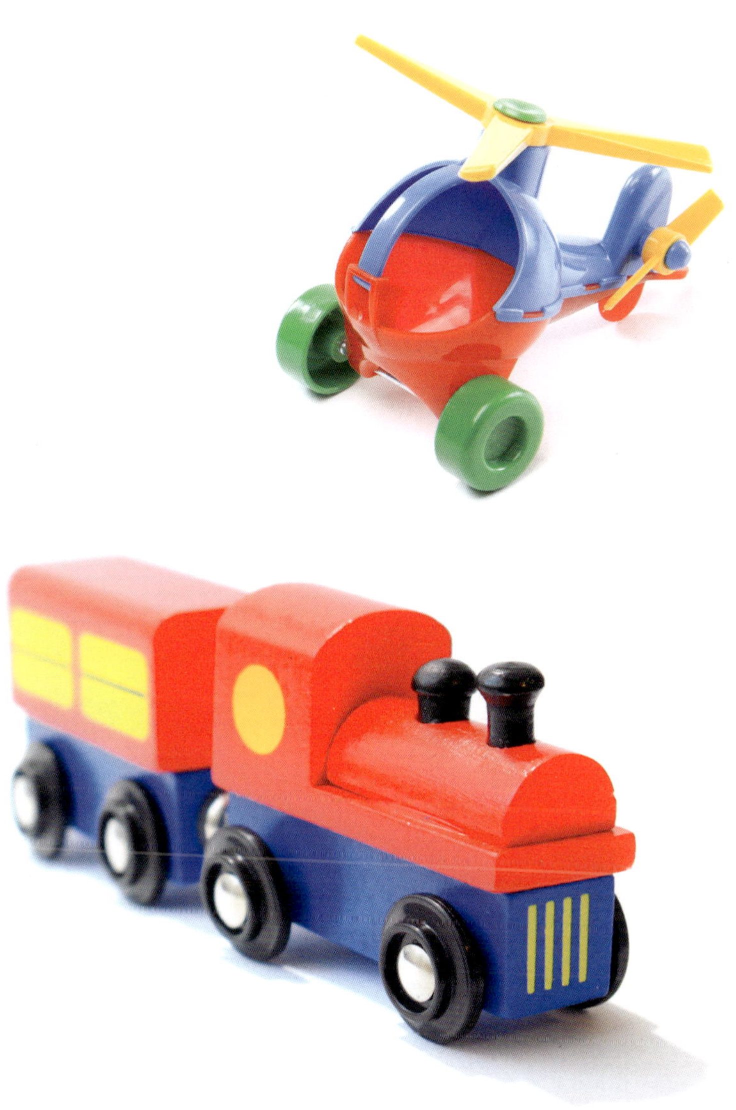

I like to give hearts.

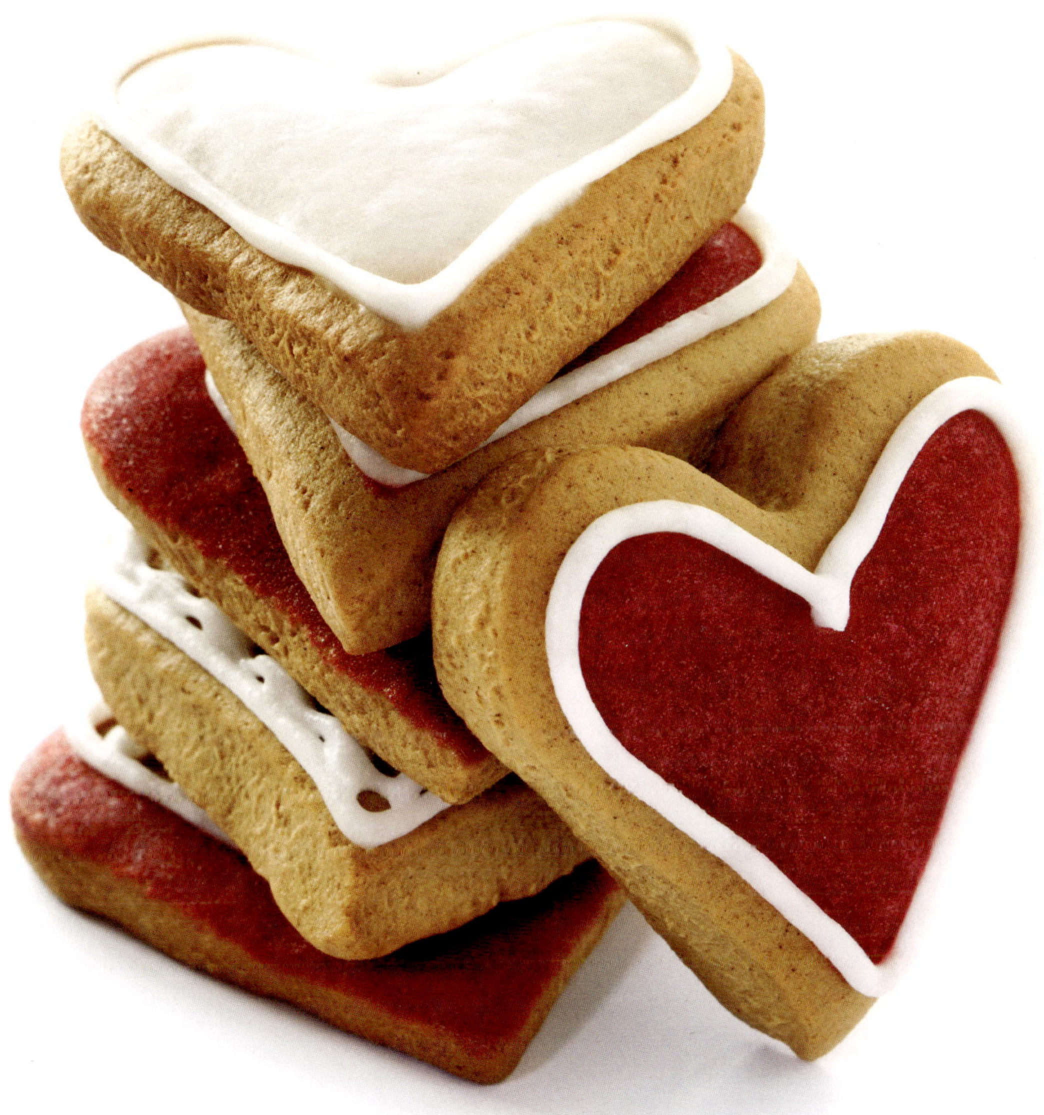

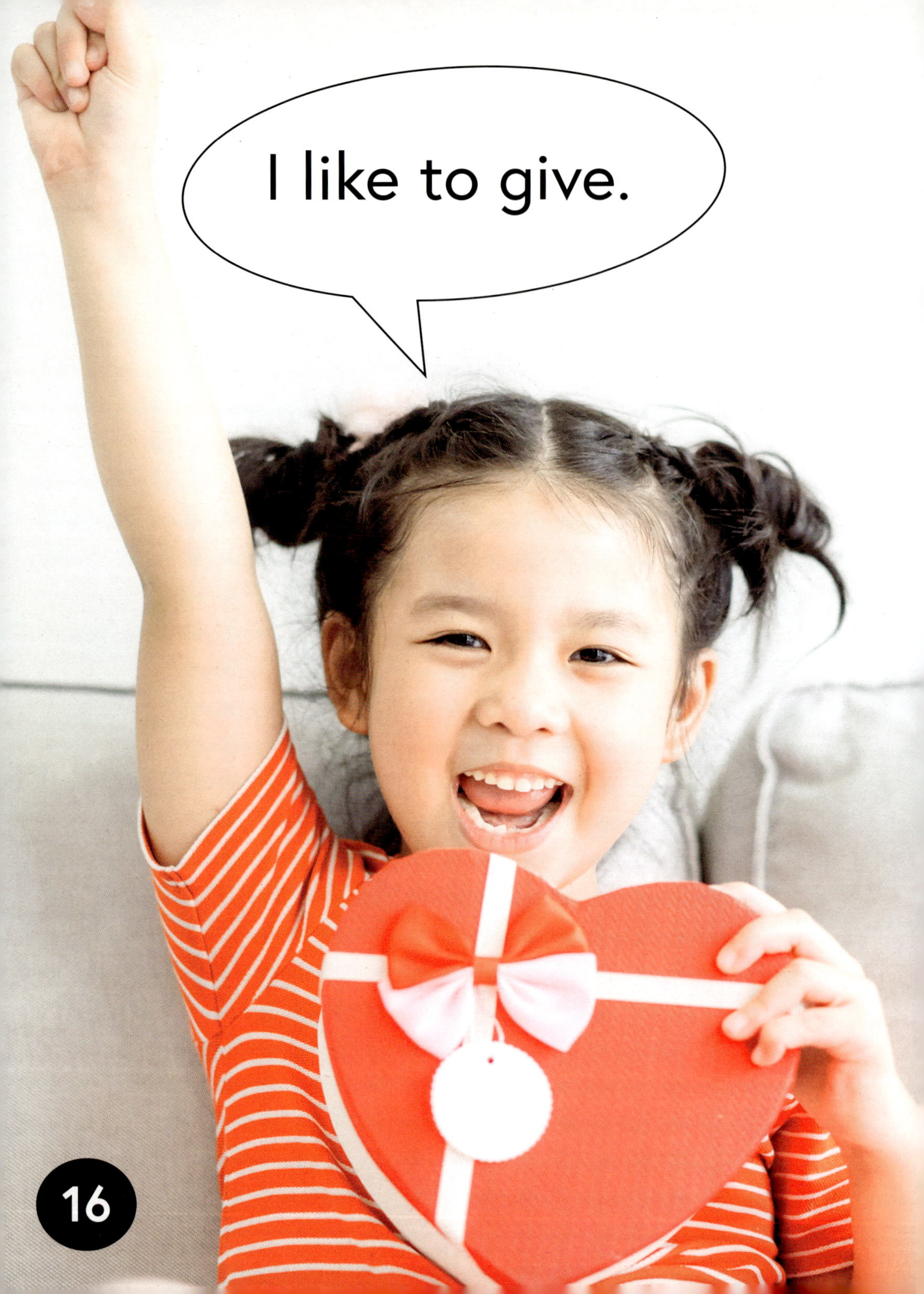
I like to give.